This book is published strictly for historical purposes.
The Naval and Military Press Ltd
expressly bears no responsibility or liability of any type,
to any first, second or third party, for any harm,
injury or loss whatsoever.

SELF-DEFENCE;

OR,

THE ART OF BOXING.

With Illustrations,

SHOWING THE VARIOUS BLOWS, STOPS AND GUARDS.

By NED DONNELLY,

Professor of Boxing to the London Athletic Club, &c., &c.

The Naval & Military Press Ltd

Published by

The Naval & Military Press Ltd
Unit 5 Riverside, Brambleside
Bellbrook Industrial Estate
Uckfield, East Sussex
TN22 1QQ England

Tel: +44 (0)1825 749494

www.naval-military-press.com
www.nmarchive.com

*In reprinting in facsimile from the original, any imperfections are inevitably reproduced
and the quality may fall short of modern type and cartographic standards.*

PREFACE.

In presenting to the public a book on the subject of the art which I pursue and profess, I think it necessary to explain, for the information of those who do not know me, the basis of my claim to their confidence as an authority on the noble English art of self-defence. He who would teach must first have learned; and in boxing a man learns best under the serious responsibility of actual encounters in the Prize Ring. A man who has boxed only with the gloves on, and has never had experience of a real fight, can be considered only as an amateur; though he may possibly be a good amateur. The boxer who may fairly claim to be a professional is the one who has practically encountered the dangers and the difficulties of fights with good antagonists.

The Prize Ring is now extinct. The prizes have disappeared, but the lessons remain; and I may claim public confidence on the ground that a career commenced in the Ring has been successfully continued (and still continues) in the boxing school.

At the early age of seventeen my young enthusiasm for the fistic art had already led me to commence the study of boxing; but I did not actually taste the hardships, dangers, toils, and triumphs of the Ring until 1864, when, in my twentieth year, I was matched for the first time. I was trained carefully at Barnet, and in the month of January, 1864, I met in the roped ring and there defeated Styles, of Paddington. My first fight occupied sixteen and a half minutes, and was happily finished in ten rounds. My next opponent was Tom McKelvy, whom I fought and beat in July, 1866. In this fight I fought for an hour with my right arm disabled, in consequence of my antagonist falling upon me and putting out my shoulder. Only my left arm was left to me, and upon this single weapon I had to rely. Tom Sayers was reduced to a similar condition in the immortal fight with the giant Heenan. My second fight lasted one hour and twenty-one minutes, and was finished in twenty-one rounds. Both these encounters were arranged and brought off satisfactorily under the auspices of Nat Langham.

Since my retirement from the Prize Ring I have been and still am occupied in teaching boxing, and I may fairly boast of success with my pupils. I have indeed, as I may modestly urge, been rather remarkably successful in teaching, since I have taught no less than sixteen winners of the Marquis of Queensberry's Cups. To use an old sporting phrase, "I am still to be heard of" at Mr. Waite's well-known school of arms, 19, Brewer Street, Golden Square, W., where I give lessons, and where I may be seen any day between ten and six.

The Prize Ring may be dead, but boxing is still as much alive as ever, and must always form a part of the athletic education of every young Englishman. My experience both in fighting and in teaching has led me to believe that I could render service to students with the pen, as well as with the gloves on my hands; hence this little manual of the noble art. If any of my definitions with pencil or with pen should seem to require further elucidation, I shall be happy to demonstrate in person to any pupil all and any of the glories of our art.

N. D.

22, GOLDEN SQUARE,
Removed to
19, BREWER STREET, LONDON, W.
1st *July*, 1881.

LIST OF ILLUSTRATIONS.

PLATE		PAGE
I.	Attitude	26
II.	Shaking hands	30
III.	Both men on guard	32
IV.	Breaking ground	36
V.	Side step	40
VI.	Left-hand lead off at the head without guarding	44
VII.	Right-hand guard for the head	48
VIII.	Left-hand lead off at head and guard	50
IX.	Left-hand lead off and duck	52
X.	Left-hand body blow	54
XI.	Stop for ditto	58
XII.	Guard for ditto and double lead off at body and head	60
XIII.	Right-hand body blow	62
XIV.	Stop for ditto	64
XV.	Guard for ditto	66
XVI.	A lead off at the head with the right, and guard for it	68
XVII.	Lead off with right hand at head, and duck	70
XVIII.	Left-hand counter on the head	72
XIX.	Do. do. and duck	74

LIST OF ILLUSTRATIONS.

PLATE		PAGE
XX.	Right-hand cross counter	78
XXI.	Stop for ditto .	80
XXII.	Right-hand counter	84
XXIII.	Stop for ditto	86
XXIV.	Left-hand upper cut	88
XXV.	A draw and stop for ditto	90
XXVI.	Right-hand upper cut .	92
XXVII.	A draw and stop for ditto .	94
XXVIII.	Another draw and stop for ditto .	96
XXIX.	How to prevent your antagonist from hitting after you have led off and passed over his left shoulder	98
XXX.	Slipping .	100
XXXI.	The head in chancery	102
XXXII.	To get out of chancery	104
XXXIII.	In-fighting	106
XXXIV.	Two men on guard, one with left and the other with right leg in front	109
XXXV.	Guard for right-hand lead off at head when opposed to a man who stands with right leg in front	110
XXXVI.	Duck and counter for ditto .	111
XXXVII.	Positions of the hands when hitting	117

SELF-DEFENCE;

OR,

THE ART OF BOXING.

THE Art of Boxing has been practised more or less among the two great nations of antiquity. The Greeks and Romans held it in high respect, and even the Jews did not wholly eschew the art of smiting, while the descendants of the Tribes who settled in England have contributed many of the most brilliant boxers to the roll of fame. That every man who desires the development of the muscular powers of the human frame, the possession of quickness, decision, endurance, and courage, should practise boxing is a matter of necessity, since by no other means can all these qualities be so thoroughly tested and cultivated. Every man should be able to use the weapons which nature has given him to the best of his ability :—not necessarily to oppress or injure others (since the best boxers are almost invariably the least quarrelsome and overbearing persons), but to be able to defend himself from attack or oppression on the part of others. The smallest and weakest man, by assiduous practice in boxing, may make himself an antagonist by no means to be despised ; and well do we remember seeing a small, pale, slender-looking slip of a fellow give a great hulking waterman, six or eight inches taller than himself, a very wholesome thrashing at Hampton Court once for attempting to bully him out of his fare. It was beautiful to see how the little man slipped away under the arms of the big one (who was weaving and walloping them about like the sails of a windmill), propping him sharply here, there, and everywhere, until the bully, worn-out and bleeding, admitted that he had had enough, and the little one walked off without a mark, amid the cheers of the spectators. The big one was probably careful in future to deal more cautiously with his customers. Boxing has been called brutal. With persons who hold that view it is perhaps useless to argue; they look only at the worst aspect of the *means*, and entirely shut their eyes to the *object*, or better side of the question. But it may fairly be asked whether manners have improved since boxing was abolished by law; whether there is less brutality, less wife-beating and kicking, now than formerly; and whether the spectacle one so often sees, of two great hulking brutes blackguarding each other in the foulest and most filthy language, yet both afraid to hit one another from want of familiarity with the usages of combat, is an improving one? Is there less brutality, less criminal violence, often attended with fatal or nearly fatal results; less ready use of un-English and unmanly weapons and means of offence, than there was formerly? We say No, emphatically, and with certainty, *no*. In the old days, when boxing flourished, if a man had been seen ill-treating a weaker one or beating and kicking a woman, twenty men who could use their fists would have come forward promptly "to help the weak," and the brute would soon have learnt at what a risk he indulged his propensities. Now twenty men will pass by on the other side, or scuttle off down a by-street to be out of the row.

Our great fatal mistake was made in putting down what was called "prize fighting." It was *first* declared illegal,

THE ART OF BOXING. 15

and then tolerated for many years. The professors of the art being thus placed under a social ban, and having to practise it in opposition to the law, the more respectable and better class of their patrons became gradually weeded out, and while the Tom Springs and Deaf Burkes, men of sterling worth, courage, and unimpeachable honesty, passed away, worse came in their places; and then this, the natural result of such a course of treatment, was pointed to as a reason for active interference and putting fighting down altogether. Yet the native love of seeing a well *stricken* field was never so strongly displayed as when Tom Sayers and Heenan fought their well-contested fight, and the best blood in England stood by the ring side and looked on with breathless interest. Had such patronage always awaited the Ring, had endeavours been made to raise its status and social condition instead of lowering it; had it been recognised as a national benefit that the youth of England should know how to protect itself, should know how to bear exertion and pain with unflinching courage and endurance; had it been admitted that a school for the encouragement and practice of the art in which the highest efficiency could be obtained was a national requisite, then indeed we should have had matters placed on a different footing, and the rowdyism and blackguardism one used to hear so much of and which were mainly due to the low parasites and hangers on of the Ring would not have been heard of at all, for the professors of the art, seeing themselves respected, would have put all this down with a strong hand.

USEFUL HINTS IN SPARRING.

Keep your eyes open.

Abstain from biting your lips, or putting your tongue between your teeth. Very serious accidents may occur from so doing.

The mouth ought to be firmly closed. The slightest tap on the lower jaw when it is hanging loose will be remembered for long afterwards, while a more severe blow may dislocate it. The value of this piece of advice will be the more obvious to the reader if he attempts simply to shake his lower jaw when his mouth is closed and then repeat the experiment with it open.

Endeavour in sparring to let the muscles work as loosely and easily as possible. Let all your movements be light and free. Lift the feet, do not drag them. By these means you will cultivate quickness, without which knowledge is of little use in boxing.

In sparring round your adversary keep the left hand and foot in front of you, and after delivering a blow, work to your right, in order to get out of reach of his right hand.

Wrestling is not permitted in boxing.

It is a foul blow to hit below the belt.

Avoid, if possible, coming to close quarters with a man of much superior weight. In out-fighting quickness may neutralise weight, but in in-fighting the latter must always tell.

Keep the hands half open while manœuvring for hits, but close them tightly when hitting or guarding.

It may perhaps be as well to explain the somewhat technical expressions of "in-fighting" and "out-fighting."

IN-FIGHTING means half-arm hitting,

with both arms, when close to your antagonist. In in-fighting a man must rely upon his quickness in hitting and cannot pay much attention to guarding.

OUT-FIGHTING means long-arm hitting and guarding, and includes manœuvring for a hit coupled with a readiness to guard.

HITTING.

POSITION OF THE HANDS AND ARMS, &c.

In hitting make as much use as possible of your weight. The blow that is simply delivered by the action of the muscles is nothing by comparison with that which is followed and driven home by the full weight of the body. Remember also to have the hands tightly closed. In fighting this would naturally be an unnecessary caution; it is, however, a frequent occurrence to see men hit with open gloves. Besides diminishing the force of the blow, a sprained or otherwise injured hand or wrist may follow.

In the left-hand lead off at the head, the blow should be given with the upper knuckles, and in all others with the hand in the position shown in plate XXXVII.

In leading off with the *left hand at the head* the arm should be perfectly straight, with the elbow turned under and palm upwards. *Vide* plate XXXVII.

For all other blows the arm should be slightly bent, the elbow pointing outwards and the palm turned half down and inwards. *Vide* plate XXXVII.

There are four hits, viz.:

    The left hand at the head.
    The left hand at the body.
    The right hand at the head.
    The right hand at the body.

DUCKING.

Ducking consists in throwing the head on one side and at the same time slightly lowering the body, so as to allow the blow intended for the head to pass harmlessly over the shoulder. It is an excellent method of avoiding a blow, affording moreover an opportunity of delivering one, for the pupil should bear in mind never to duck without at the same time hitting. When opposed to a bigger man than yourself, fight at his body, using the ducks shown in plates X. and XIII.

There are five ducks:

The duck to the right, as practised when countering with the left hand on the head. *Vide* plate XIX.

The duck to the right, when it is intended

to deliver a left-hand body blow. *Vide* plate X.

The duck to the left while delivering a right-hand cross-counter. *Vide* plate XX.

The duck to the left, giving at the same time a right-hand body blow. *Vide* plate XIII.

The duck to the right, which is sometimes used when leading off at the head with the left hand, in order to avoid a counter. *Vide* plate IX.

FEINTING.

A feint is a false attack made to divert attention from the real danger which follows, as, for instance, a left-hand feint followed by a right-hand blow, or a feint at the head followed by a body blow. To make a feint with the left hand, straighten the arm suddenly as though you were going to deliver a blow, and at the same time advance the left foot about six inches, keeping the head back, then return to the guard.

A feint with the right hand is made thus: draw the arm back suddenly as though you were going to hit, and at the same time advance the left foot about six inches, keeping the head back, then return to the guard. "Drawing" has some affinity with feinting, and may be described under the same head. Its object is to induce your opponent to deliver a certain blow for which you are prepared, and which it is your intention to counter; you do this either by feinting and enticing him to follow you up, or by laying yourself open with apparent carelessness to the attack you wish him to make. Both are, of course, exceedingly useful, but the beginner will do well to cultivate quickness and attain some proficiency in straightforward sparring before he turns his attention to manœuvres which are more likely to get himself than his adversary into trouble if they are not performed with great rapidity. When your opponent feints or attempts to draw you, either get back or else guard both head and body as illustrated in plate VII.

STOPPING.

A stop is a time hit delivered on a man when he is leading off or preparing to do so. It requires great readiness and decision, but if given in proper time it either stops the intended attack or prevents it from reaching you with any force.

All the hits made when ducking may be stopped by a left-hand blow on the face.

A stop may also be made with the right hand, but is not so certain as when made with the left.

PLATE I.—ATTITUDE.

PLATE I.

ATTITUDE.

In this position the toes of the right foot must be directly behind and in a line with the left heel. The distance between the feet naturally varies according to the height; for a man of 5 ft. 8 in. it should be 14 inches. Let the right foot be turned slightly out, and raise the heel about two inches from the ground; the weight then will rest on the ball of the foot. The left foot ought to be flat on the ground and pointed towards your opponent's left toe. Slightly bend both knees. The right arm should be across the "màrk" (that point where the ribs begin to arch), the hand being an inch below the left breast. To obtain the exact position of the left arm, advance the left shoulder, drop the arm by the side and then raise the fore-arm until the hand is on a level with the elbow. In sparring it should be worked easily forward and backward. Throw the right shoulder well back, and slightly sink it, so that of the two the left shoulder is the higher. Lower the chin, turn the face a little to the right, and bend the head slightly over the right shoulder. The object of turning the face is to prevent both eyes being hit at once, while the head is bent to the right in order that it may not be directly in a line with your opponent's left hand, and thus afford him an easy target.

BOXING GLOVES AND HOW TO PUT THEM ON.

In the preceding illustration no gloves are on the hands, in order to show the position of the fingers and thumbs when the hands are clenched for hitting, but in practice, gloves should always be worn.

The best gloves for boxing are Frank Bryan's Registered "Champion" gloves, the hands of which are made of soft leather and ventilated in the palms, the backs of dressed sheepskin (commonly called kid), stuffed with hair.

They should be kept clean and dry. Should any dirt get on these gloves, it is easily washed off with a sponge and a little soap and water.

Wash-leather gloves prickle the face and make it sore, and are not so easily cleaned.

When you put the gloves on, push your hands well into them, so that you can shut your hands when hitting or guarding.

PLATE II.—SHAKING HANDS.

PLATE II.

SHAKING HANDS.

Both before and after a bout with the gloves, the combatants should thus salute one another. It is a good old-fashioned English custom, betokening friendly feeling, and should never be omitted. A hearty shake of the hands after a warm set-to, in which both men have perhaps become rather more earnest than is necessary, at once dissipates what might otherwise grow into ill-feeling. As the hand is extended, move the right foot to the front, and at the conclusion of the ceremony throw it smartly behind the left and assume at once the position given in plate I.

PLATE III.—BOTH MEN ON GUARD.

PLATE III.

BOTH MEN ON GUARD.

It is of the utmost importance that a man should stand and get about well. The advantage of quick hands is sadly neutralised by slow legs. To get about quickly and safely, there must be some arrangement and method in the steps. An experienced boxer, who has paid attention to the action of the feet, always stands firmly; his feet are never flurried, the same distance usually separates them; he moves rapidly, neatly, and quietly. With a novice, or boxer who imagines that getting about is an unimportant detail, and the manner in which he moves of no consequence, the case is different. As a rule his movements are few and deplorably

c

slow; when suddenly attacked he loses his balance, and most of his attention is consequently directed to saving himself from falling. Should he, however, be more ambitious, and attempt to move with any rapidity, the whole performance is a scramble. His feet are too close together, or too far apart, his legs are (if I may use such an expression) constantly in his way; he stumbles, staggers, and rolls about in an absurd manner, not unfrequently ending by tripping himself up, and falling even without the assistance of a blow.

By referring to the plate you will see both men on guard, in the position illustrated in plate No. I., and before proceeding further they should practise the following steps:—

To advance, move the left foot about ten inches forward, placing it upon the ground heel first. Let the right foot follow it the same distance. Bear in mind that the space between the feet should vary as little as possible.

To retire, step back about ten inches with the right foot, following it in like manner with the left.

To take ground to the right, move the left foot about twelve inches to the right, following it immediately with the right, and assuming again position No. I.

To take ground to the left, move the right foot twelve inches to the left, and place the left directly in front of it.

By adopting these steps the right foot is always behind the left, you are always in position, and consequently ready either for attack or defence.

PLATE IV.—BREAKING GROUND.

PLATE IV.

BREAKING GROUND.

This is the term applied to the usual method of retreat in boxing. You break ground in the following manner. In leading off at the head your right foot will be raised from the ground (*vide* plate VII.). As you set it down again and the weight of the body is transferred to it from the left leg, spring backwards, letting the left foot touch the ground first, and alighting on the same spot upon which you formerly placed the right, which then assumes its natural position in the rear. You will thus find yourself in position a pace behind the spot from which you originally stepped in to lead off. It is necessary sometimes, if your opponent follows you up very quickly, to double the step, that is to say, to make two consecutive springs backwards. For other blows, although the right foot is not raised from the ground at the moment of striking, the movements in breaking ground are precisely the same, for the moment the weight falls on the right leg you spring back as described above.

TO PRACTISE BREAKING GROUND.

Place yourself at the end of a room with your face to the wall, in the position you would be at the moment of striking in a lead off at the head with the left hand. Your right foot will then be off the ground.

Make as many consecutive springs backwards in a direct line to your rear as the room will permit, keeping the knees slightly bent, the left toes pointing to your front, and the arms placed as shown in plate I.

The feet should fall lightly on the ground, and all the joints, particularly those of the legs, should be held loose.

PLATE V.—SIDE STEP.

PLATE V.

SIDE STEP.

This is exceedingly useful in avoiding a rush or in getting away when you are driven back against the ropes. We will suppose you to be in position facing your adversary. By a sudden movement of the feet, half spring, half step, you turn the body to the right, change the relative position of the legs, and assume the attitude of a fencer on the lunge, that is, with the right instead of the left leg in front, as is usual in boxing. Your left should now be turned towards your adversary, the line of your feet being at right angles to the line in which they formerly stood. The left foot should be upon almost the same spot formerly occupied by your right. If your adversary advances hastily and without caution whilst you are in this posture he will be apt to trip over your left leg. Bring the left foot into position before the right, and you will then stand a pace to the right of your original station. If this step is executed rapidly you elude your opponent, for he will no longer be in front of you, and consequently you can easily get away from the ropes. A combination of the side step and breaking ground should also be practised. Spring back as if breaking ground, and alight in the posture above described as that of a fencer on the lunge, with the body turned to the right, bring the left foot into position before the right, and you thus get back and work to the right of yourself at the same time.

KEEPING THE ELBOWS IN.

Before proceeding to describe the various hits, &c., it will not be out of place here to impress upon the mind of the boxer how necessary it is to keep the elbows close to the sides while manœuvring. By doing so, your body is better covered when on guard, you are much readier for hitting, and you are enabled to hit straighter, quicker, and with more force. A man who spars with his elbows stuck out makes two motions with his arm, instead of one, in leading off, as he has to bring his elbow into line before delivering.

PLATE VI.—LEFT-HAND LEAD OFF AT THE HEAD WITHOUT GUARDING.

PLATE VI.

LEFT-HAND LEAD OFF AT THE HEAD WITHOUT GUARDING.

The lead off at the head should, as a rule, be made with the left hand. Its importance can hardly be exaggerated. Every effort should therefore be directed towards attaining proficiency in this particular. A quick lead off frequently enables a man to score point after point without receiving a return. He spars round his adversary, watching for an opportunity, and then, having measured his distance well, steps in, plants a blow, and is away again at once. With these tactics at his command, a light man will often fight a heavy weight all over without coming to close quarters, at which weight would inevitably tell in favour of its possessor. A slow lead off lays a man open to counters and cross-counters, which will hereafter be described.

The lead off should be made when the hand is in the position shown in plate I. In all other blows the hand is more or less drawn back before delivery; in this case, however, it should come straight out, as it were spontaneously, and without the slightest hesitation. Beginners are almost always inclined to hit downwards, or "chop" and bear heavily upon their opponent's guard. This should be avoided. In stepping in push yourself off the ball of the right foot, and spring in about eighteen inches. The action of foot and arm should be simultaneous; do not step in and then deliver the blow. The lead off at the head with the left hand is the only blow that is delivered while the right foot is raised from the ground.

As you step in the right foot should follow, and, at the moment of striking, hang over the spot formerly occupied by the left. Full advantage is thus taken of height and reach. Be careful when you step in to place the left foot upon the ground, heel first. If the toe touches the ground first, and your adversary by chance gets back instead of guarding or receiving your blow, you do not meet with the expected resistance, and consequently are apt to overbalance; in which case, until you can recover yourself, you are at his mercy. The head and right hand remain in position No. I.

PLATE VII.—RIGHT-HAND GUARD FOR THE HEAD.

PLATE VII.

RIGHT-HAND GUARD FOR THE HEAD.

To guard the head from your opponent's left hand, raise the right hand nearly to a level and in front of the left temple. Let the fore-arm cross the face, and be thrown forward so as to turn instead of receiving the weight of the blow. Keep the elbow down. Close the hand firmly in order to brace the sinews, and turn the palm partly outward, or the blow will fall on the bone of the arm instead of the muscle. At the same time bend the head forward and to the right—thus, although the face is well out of danger, you can still see your opponent over the fore-arm.

When sparring with a man who chops, that is, hits downwards, do not guard his lead off, or you will get your arm severely punished, but avoid it by quickly retiring, keeping your hands perfectly still. Then instantly he has delivered his blow, in which his hand will naturally fall, step in and strike out with your left at his face

PLATE VIII.—LEFT-HAND LEAD OFF AT HEAD AND GUARD.

PLATE VIII.

LEFT-HAND LEAD OFF AT HEAD AND GUARD.

This lead off is precisely the same as that shown in plate VI., except that as you deliver the blow you throw up the right-hand guard to protect the face from a possible left hand counter. It requires a little practice to do this without detracting from the rapidity of your lead off; your trouble will however be well spent, for with an opponent who frequently attempts left-hand counters this will be found a very useful manœuvre.

A LEFT-HAND FEINT AND LEAD OFF.

Feint a lead off with the left hand, so as to induce your adversary to throw up his right-hand guard. Should he do so, hit at the pit of the stomach. Should he not raise his right hand, follow the feint up with a genuine lead off at the head.

(*Continued on page* 53.)

PLATE IX.—LEFT-HAND LEAD OFF AND DUCK.

Particular attention should be paid in this attack to the action of the feet. Make a short step with the left foot (about six inches) as though you were going to lead off, then withdraw it and suddenly deliver the blow; using the feet as described in plates VI. and X. This movement requires some practice, as it should be performed with great rapidity.

PLATE IX.

LEFT-HAND LEAD OFF AND DUCK.

This illustration represents the same lead off again. In place of the right-hand guard, it is, however, accompanied with a duck, thus avoiding instead of guarding the left-hand counter. Observe that for this blow the right foot is not raised; it does not follow the left as in the preceding examples, but remains firmly planted on the ground, as in the left hand body blow.

PLATE X.—LEFT-HAND BODY BLOW.

PLATE X.

LEFT-HAND BODY BLOW.

This blow should never be attempted unless you are confident that you have sufficient room behind you to be able to get well away again. It should be directed at the pit of the stomach, which is the weakest part of the body. Occasionally it may with advantage be preceded by a feint at the head, in order to induce your opponent to throw up his right-hand guard and lay the "mark" open. Let the ball of the right foot be kept well on the ground. Step in with the left foot, until the feet are about thirty inches apart, hitting out at the same time and ducking to the right. In the event of your adversary attempting to counter you with the left, your head will thus be outside his arm, which will pass harmlessly over your left shoulder. For this blow the arm should be slightly bent, the elbow turned out, and the palm of the hand turned inwards and partly down. The right arm should in the meantime be drawn back seven or eight inches, and the glove held close to the side. To get away, turn the left heel outwards and spring well back, taking care not to raise the head until out of distance.

DOUBLE LEAD OFF AT BODY AND HEAD.

Commence with the body blow as described in No. X.; instead, though, of retiring immediately you have struck out, bring the right foot about twelve inches forward, step in a few inches with the left, and follow the first blow up with a second aimed at the face. Both blows, which must follow one another as rapidly as possible, should be delivered with the left hand. The palm in each instance ought to be turned down.

PLATE XI.—STOP FOR LEFT-HAND BODY BLOW.

PLATE XI.

STOP FOR LEFT-HAND BODY BLOW.

Like all stops, this requires very accurate timing. Having foreseen your adversary's intention, hit him full in the face with your left hand before he can get his head down. Keep your right arm in its original position across the "mark."

PLATE XII.—GUARD FOR LEFT-HAND BODY BLOW AND DOUBLE LEAD OFF AT BODY AND HEAD.

PLATE XII.

GUARD FOR LEFT-HAND BODY BLOW AND DOUBLE LEAD OFF AT BODY AND HEAD.

To guard the left-hand body blow, throw the left arm across the mark, and at the same time put up the right-hand guard, so that should your adversary attempt to make the double lead off at the body and head you are completely guarded. Be careful to hold the left arm firmly against the body, for even the jar of a severe body blow will knock a good deal of the wind out of a man. Step back about six inches with the right foot, so as to be better able to resist a rush.

PLATE XIII.—RIGHT-HAND BODY BLOW.

PLATE XIII.

RIGHT-HAND BODY BLOW.

This should be aimed at a little below the heart. It is delivered under the same circumstances and in the same manner as the left-hand body blow (*vide* No. X.), with these exceptions: you duck to the left instead of right, and the feet when you have stepped in should only be twenty inches apart instead of thirty; you have consequently to get nearer your opponent before attempting it. Be sure always that you have sufficient room behind you for retreat.

Should he attempt to put his left arm round your neck while you are delivering this blow, duck to your right under his arm and get away. This should always be done when a man attempts to seize your head. When opposed to a man who stands with the right leg in front, you must duck to your left.

PLATE XIV.—STOP FOR RIGHT-HAND BODY BLOW.

PLATE XIV.

STOP FOR RIGHT-HAND BODY BLOW.

This stop is exactly the same as that recommended for the left-hand body blow. *Vide* No. XI.

PLATE XV.—GUARD FOR RIGHT-HAND BODY BLOW.

PLATE XV.

GUARD FOR RIGHT-HAND BODY BLOW.

Bring the left side forward and drop the left arm, which should be slightly bent, so as to cover the side and front of the thigh. Care should be taken to press the arm close to the body, in order to prevent the jar through which you would otherwise feel much of the force of the blow.

HOW TO AVOID A LEAD OFF AT THE BODY WITH EITHER HAND.

As your adversary attacks, retire a step, which will take you out of distance, then as he is recovering to his guard, step in and deliver a left-hand hit at his face.

PLATE XVI.—A LEAD OFF AT THE HEAD WITH THE RIGHT, AND GUARD FOR IT.

PLATE XVI.

A LEAD OFF AT THE HEAD WITH THE RIGHT, AND GUARD FOR IT.

Feint with the left, then bring in the right hand, aiming it at the chin or angle of the jaw.

GUARD FOR LEAD OFF AT THE HEAD WITH THE RIGHT.

Raise the left elbow and bend the arm so that the fist is somewhat lower and nearer to the body than the elbow. Let the palm be turned to the front. Shift the right foot back about six inches, and lean a little forward, so that you are the better able to resist the attack. Look over your wrist, and receive the blow upon the elbow.

ANOTHER LEAD OFF AT THE HEAD WITH THE RIGHT.

Feint with the left, hitting your opponent
(*Continued on page 71.*)

PLATE XVII.—LEAD OFF WITH RIGHT HAND AT HEAD, AND DUCK.

on the right arm. Do not withdraw your hand, but as he raises his guard rest upon it with your left and pin it to his chest; then bring in the right hand, aiming it at the chin or angle of the jaw. Properly delivered this is a most punishing blow, for by steadying yourself with the left hand you can bring your full force into play with the right.

PLATE XVII.

LEAD OFF WITH RIGHT HAND AT HEAD AND DUCK.

When leading off at the head with the right, you may duck to the left, and avoid a right-hand counter. In this illustration both men are performing this manœuvre.

PLATE XVIII.—LEFT-HAND COUNTER ON THE HEAD.

PLATE XVIII.

LEFT-HAND COUNTER ON THE HEAD.

This happens when two men lead off at the head with the left hand at the same time.

PLATE XIX.—LEFT-HAND COUNTER ON THE HEAD, AND DUCK.

PLATE XIX.

LEFT-HAND COUNTER ON THE HEAD, AND DUCK.

There are perhaps few blows more unpleasantly startling than a good left-hand counter which meets you full face. It opens a spacious firmament to the bewildered eyes, wherein you discover more new planets in a second than the most distinguished astronomer ever observed in a life-time. As your adversary leads off at your head with his left hand, duck to the right so as to allow his blow to pass over your left shoulder; step in about twelve inches and strike out at his face. The right foot should not be moved. Here both men have, as it happens, made use of the same stratagem; in consequence of which, both left arms have passed harmlessly over each other's left shoulder.

LEFT-HAND COUNTER ON THE HEAD, AND GUARD.

The difference between this and the preceding counter will be easily understood by studying the plate. It consists simply in guarding your opponent's lead off instead of ducking to avoid it. You step in and hit out as before.

LEFT-HAND COUNTER ON THE BODY.

This should be delivered when your adversary is leading off at your head with his left hand. Duck to the right, step in about twelve inches, and aim your blow at the pit of his stomach. The right hand should be drawn seven or eight inches back and held close to the side. To get away, turn the left heel out and spring well back. Do **not** raise the head until out of distance.

PLATE XX.—RIGHT-HAND CROSS COUNTER.

PLATE XX.

RIGHT-HAND CROSS COUNTER.

This is the most severe blow which can be dealt in sparring. It is delivered as follows:—As your opponent leads off at your head with his left hand, step in about twelve inches, ducking to the left, at the same time shooting your right hand across his left arm and shoulder. The blow should be aimed either at the angle of the jaw or chin, and the palm of the hand should be half turned down. Let both feet be turned slightly to the left, as by these means the right side is brought forward, and greater force given to the blow. As the counter is delivered, draw the left hand back to the position illustrated in the plate, then, should a second blow be necessary, before getting away you can deliver it.

PLATE XXI.—STOP FOR RIGHT-HAND CROSS COUNTER.

PLATE XXI.

STOP FOR RIGHT-HAND CROSS COUNTER.

Anticipating your adversary's intention, hit him full in the face with the left hand before he ducks; or, instead of striking at his face, deliver the blow on the right side of his chest near to the shoulder, and his right hand will be effectually stopped.

ANOTHER STOP FOR RIGHT-HAND CROSS COUNTER.

As you lead off with your left drop the head well forward, so that at the end of the movement your left ear will be touching the inside of your upper arm, when the angle of your jaw and chin will be completely covered by your shoulder.

F

Body blows with left or right hand will act as stops for all right-hand hits at the head.

PLATE XXII.—RIGHT-HAND COUNTER.

PLATE XXII.

RIGHT-HAND COUNTER.

This occurs when both men lead off together with the right hand.

PLATE XXIII.—STOP FOR RIGHT-HAND COUNTER.

PLATE XXIII.

STOP FOR RIGHT-HAND COUNTER.

Duck your head to the left as you lead off.

RIGHT-HAND COUNTER ON THE BODY.

Duck to the left in order to avoid your opponent's lead off, and strike out with the right hand at a point a little below the heart. The left hand should be drawn back as shown in the illustration. In all other particulars this blow represents the preceding. For this and the left-hand counter, it will be well to study the right and left-hand body blows (Nos. XIII. and X.), for, with the exception of the circumstances under which they are delivered, and the difference in the distance of the advance made, the blows are the same.

PLATE XXIV.—LEFT-HAND UPPER CUT.

PLATE XXIV.

LEFT-HAND UPPER CUT.

This blow, which in reality is a counter, should be given when a man in leading off at your head with his left hand holds his head down. Guard your face with the right arm, step in about twelve inches, and hit upwards with the left. The arm should be bent and elbow turned down. The force of the blow must come in a great measure from the body.

PLATE XXV.—DRAW AND STOP FOR LEFT-HAND UPPER CUT.

PLATE XXV.

DRAW AND STOP FOR LEFT-HAND UPPER CUT.

Feint a lead off at your opponent's face with your head down, then duck to the right, and give the left-hand body blow as described in No. X.

PLATE XXVI.—RIGHT-HAND UPPER CUT.

PLATE XXVI.

RIGHT-HAND UPPER CUT.

With this exception that you do not guard, this blow is similar to and delivered under the same circumstances as the left-hand upper cut. In delivering it the head should be slightly bent to the left.

PLATE XXVII.—A DRAW AND STOP FOR RIGHT-HAND UPPER CUT.

PLATE XXVII.

A DRAW AND STOP FOR RIGHT-HAND UPPER CUT.

Feint with the head as if it were your intention to lead off with it down, then throw the head back and lead off at your adversary's face with the left hand.

PLATE XXVIII.—ANOTHER DRAW AND STOP FOR RIGHT-HAND UPPER CUT.

PLATE XXVIII.

ANOTHER DRAW AND STOP FOR RIGHT-HAND UPPER CUT.

Feint a lead off at your opponent's face with your left hand, then duck to the left and put in the right-hand body blow. The reader should notice in this, as in other illustrations, the position of the hand not absolutely in use. Never drop your hands until out of distance.

PLATE XXIX.—HOW TO PREVENT YOUR ANTAGONIST FROM HITTING AFTER YOU HAVE LED OFF AND PASSED OVER HIS LEFT SHOULDER.

PLATE XXIX.

HOW TO PREVENT YOUR ANTAGONIST FROM HITTING AFTER YOU HAVE LED OFF AND PASSED OVER HIS LEFT SHOULDER.

When this occurs, bend the elbow quickly, place your fore-arm against his throat, and thrust his head back. Grasp his left shoulder with your left hand and seize his left elbow with your right hand. This will effectually stop him from hitting you.

PLATE XXX.—SLIPPING.

PLATE XXX.

SLIPPING.

This is an exceedingly useful manœuvre, which enables you to avoid a rush or get out of a corner. Feint a lead off, tapping your adversary lightly on the chest or right arm; do not then retire, but as he comes at you duck to the right, make another step forward (as described in double lead off at body and head), and pass under his left arm. To face him again turn to the left.

PLATE XXXI.—THE HEAD IN CHANCERY.

PLATE XXXI.

THE HEAD IN CHANCERY.

No directions can be given for getting a man into this position. When in close quarters you should, however, always be on the look out for a chance of doing so. If it occurs, grasp your opponent firmly round the neck with the left arm and use the right to punish him.

PLATE XXXII.—TO GET OUT OF CHANCERY.

PLATE XXXII.

TO GET OUT OF CHANCERY.

Almost the best advice to give a man who is firmly and fairly caught in chancery is not to attempt to get out, at least unless the hold loosens, and he can make his effort with some chance of success. In pulling away or resisting he is simply hanging himself. He should, therefore, push his opponent back (see plate XXXI.), and at the same time fight to the best of his ability with both hands. If, however, he discovers the danger before the grasp has tightened, he should place one hand under his adversary's fore-arm near the elbow, the other under the shoulder, and push the arm up, ducking at the same time, and dragging the head away.

PLATE XXXIII.—IN FIGHTING.

have it, keep this advantage. Aim the left hand at the eyes and nose, the right at the chin or angle of the jaw. After delivering five or six blows, get away. Never fight at the body in in-fighting, invariably make the head your mark.

PLATE XXXIV.—TWO MEN ON GUARD, ONE WITH LEFT AND THE OTHER WITH RIGHT LEG IN FRONT.

PLATE XXXIII.

IN-FIGHTING.

In-fighting generally takes place in a corner or near the side of the ring. In in-fighting bring the right foot forward until it is nearly in a line with the left, drop the chin and lean forward so as to receive the blows on the forehead. Keep your eyes fixed on your antagonist Use both hands and hit rapidly, bringing the shoulder well forward at each blow. The arms should not be drawn too far back, as time is lost thereby; a great deal of the force of the blow is obtained by turning the body slightly to right or left as you hit. It is a great advantage to have your hands inside your opponent's; you should therefore keep them as close together as possible, so as to obtain, or if you already

PLATE XXXV.—GUARD FOR RIGHT-HAND LEAD OFF AT HEAD WHEN OPPOSED TO A MAN WHO STANDS WITH RIGHT LEG IN FRONT.

PLATE XXXVI.—DUCK AND COUNTER FOR A LEAD OFF AT HEAD BY A MAN WHO STANDS WITH RIGHT LEG IN FRONT.

THE WAY TO DEAL WITH A MAN WHO STANDS WITH HIS RIGHT LEG AND RIGHT ARM IN FRONT.

Work to your left in order to avoid his left hand. Be chary in leading off with the left hand, as that is at once difficult and dangerous. It is far better to lead off with the right hand and duck at the same time to the left. When your adversary leads off with the right hand, duck to the left and counter either upon the face or body.

The blow on the face must be given like the right cross counter (*vide* plate XX.) and the one on the body like the right-hand body blow shown in plate XIII., except that you must aim at the pit of the stomach instead of at a little below the heart.

THE GUARDS FOR AN OPPONENT WHO STANDS WITH HIS RIGHT LEG IN FRONT.

When he leads off with the right-hand guard with the left-arm, as shown in plate XXXV., guard his left with your right arm, as shown in plate VII.

Use the guards illustrated in plates XV. and XII. for his right and left hand body blows, guarding his right with your left and his left with your right.

Avoid in-fighting with him as much as possible.

I have now, to the best of my ability, described the principal hits, stops, guards, &c., in boxing, as I use and teach them myself. Having to a certain extent perfected himself in these, the pupil will do well to go through the following exercises, making the hits as smartly and as rapidly in succession as possible, but not omitting to return to the position illustrated in plate No. I. after each blow. The opponents should take it in turns to guard and attack.

1st Exercise.

1.—Left-hand body blow (get back).
2.—Right-hand blow (get back).
3.—Left-hand lead off at the head, guarding with the right (get back).
4.—Right-hand cross counter (get back).
5.—Lead off at the head with the left and duck to the right (get back).

2nd Exercise.

1.—Right-hand body blow (get back).
2.—Lead off with the left at the head without guarding (get back).
3.—Right-hand cross counter (get back).
4.—Left-hand body blow (get back).
5.—Lead off with the left at the head and duck (get back).

3RD EXERCISE.

1.—Lead off with the left hand at the head without guarding (get back).
2.—Right-hand cross counter (get back).
3.—Left-hand lead off at the head and duck to the right (get back).
4.—Left-hand body blow (get back).
5.—Right-hand body blow (get back).

4TH EXERCISE.

1.—Lead off with left at body, then make a short step in and repeat the blow on the face (get back). (*This is the double lead off at body and head*, vide *page* 31.)
2.—Lead off with left and right at head (get back).
3.—As your opponent retires, advance quickly, then step in and deliver the left on the face (get back).

4.—Both men lead off with left and guard (get back).

5TH EXERCISE.

1.—Lead off with the left hand at the head (get back).
2.—Right-hand cross counter, remain and commence in-fighting, deliver five or six blows and get back.

Never degenerate into a rough, unmeaning, unscientific scramble. In the midst of impetuosity remember coolness; and never let the heat of action lead you to forget good temper. Be manly; seek no undue advantage. Science and pluck give advantage enough.

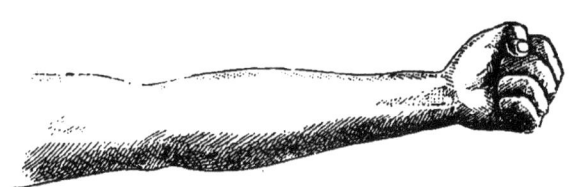

LEFT-HAND LEAD OFF AT HEAD.

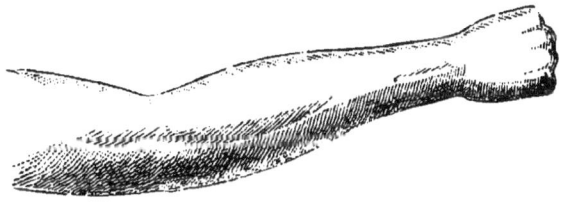

RIGHT-HAND CROSS COUNTER.

LEFT-HAND BODY BLOW.

RIGHT-HAND BODY BLOW.

PLATE XXXVII.—POSITIONS OF THE HANDS WHEN HITTING.

BOXING COMPETITIONS.

In boxing competitions there should be four judges, a referee, and timekeeper; a judge to sit at each corner of the ring (outside), and the referee to move about so that he may see the whole of the manœuvring and hitting, and at the end of each round the referee and judges should assemble and decide, during the interval between the rounds, which man has had the advantage. When the judges sit together, they cannot possibly see all the hits given.

The competitors should toss for corners.

The referee should under no circumstances be the timekeeper, as he cannot both keep time and watch the rounds.

In judging, both body and head blows, indeed, all the points in boxing, should be taken into consideration, as well as form and style.

In-fighting should not be ignored and looked upon as roughing. There is great art in it, and in a street fight it is much more useful than out-fighting.

The competitors should be divided into four weights, termed "Feather," "Light," "Middle," and "Heavy," viz. :—

Feather for men under 8 stone.
Light   ,,   10 ,,
Middle   ,,   11 st. 4 lb.

Heavy for men of any weight.

Three rounds should be sparred, the first and second of three minutes' duration each, and the third of four minutes. A minute allowed between the rounds.

In striking, the blow *must* be delivered with the hand closed.

The seconds should not be allowed to be

in the ring, except during intervals between the rounds, neither should they be permitted to direct their men during a round, either by word or sign.

When a competitor draws a bye, he should invariably be compelled to spar three rounds of the same duration as the others.

No competitor should be allowed to lay hold of the ropes to assist him in the contest.

Any competitor who may be disabled during a round, and not be able to renew the contest before sixty seconds have expired, shall be considered beaten.

HOW TO PITCH A RING.

The ground should be level, and where there is sufficient room the ring should be 24 feet square, formed of two lines of ropes and eight stakes.

The stakes should be strong, with round tops, and have holes or rings through which to run the ropes, and should be firmly fixed in the ground, out of which they should stand 5 feet.

Two rows of ropes of 4 inches in circumference should be run round the ring, the bottom one about 2 feet 3 inches from the ground, and the top one 4 feet 3 inches.

When the ring is on a raised stage, a stout piece of wood about 5 or 6 inches deep should be fixed all round the edge of the floor to prevent the men slipping off.

Under no circumstances should the ring be less than 12 feet square. In a ring of less dimensions the men would not have sufficient room to use their feet, without which there can be no good boxing.

WINNERS

OF

THE MARQUIS OF QUEENSBERRY'S

BOXING CHAMPIONSHIP CUPS

Since the Commencement of the Competitions.

HEAVY WEIGHTS.—(Any Weight.)

1867. J. C. HALLIDAY.
1868. T. MILVAIN.
1869. No competition.
1870. H. J. CHINNERY.
1871. H. J. CHINNERY.
1872. E. B. MICHELL.
1873. F. B. MADDISON.
1874. D. GIBSON.
1875. A. L. HIGHTON.

1876. R. WAKEFIELD.
1877. J. M. R. FRANCIS.
1878. R. FROST SMITH.
1879. G. H. VIZE.
1880. R. FROST-SMITH.
1881. G. FRYER.
1882. A. F. SOMERSET.
1883. LT. MONTGOMERIE.
1884. W. A. J. WEST.

MIDDLE WEIGHTS.—(11 st. 4 lbs. and under.)

1867. H. J. CHINNERY.
1868. H. J. CHINNERY.
1869. H. J. CHINNERY.
1870. E. B. MICHELL.
1871. E. C. STREATFIELD.
1872. H. J. BLYTH.
1873. A. WALKER.
1874. F. R. THOMAS.
1875. J. H. DOUGLAS.

1876. J. H. DOUGLAS.
1877. J. H. DOUGLAS.
1878. G. I. GARLAND.
1879. H. G. BRINSMEAD.
1880. W. B. BARGE.
1881. P. BELLHOUSE.
1882. F. FRANCIS.
1883. S. H. REED
1884. H. J. KINLOCH.

LIGHT WEIGHTS.—(10 st. and under.)

1867. R. CLEMINSON.
1868. No competition.
1869. H. L. JEYES, w. o.
1870. R. V. CHURTON.
1871. R. V. CHURTON.
1872. R. V. CHURTON.
1873. C. T. HOBBS.
1874. L. DÉNÉRÉAZ.
1875. H. S. GILES.
1876. A. BULTITUDE.
1877. H. SKEATE.
1878. G. AIREY.
1879. G. AIREY.
1880. E. HUTCHINGS.
1881. E. B. MICHELL.
1882. C. H. KAIN.
1883. H. J. HOWLETT.
1884. W. HUTCHINGS.

WINNERS

OF THE

AMATEUR BOXING ASSOCIATION'S CHAMPIONSHIP CUPS.

HEAVY WEIGHTS.

1881. R. FROST SMITH.
1882. H. T. DEARSLEY.
1883. H. T. DEARSLEY.
1884. H. T. DEARSLEY.

MIDDLE WEIGHTS.

1881. P. BELLHOUSE.
1882. A. H. KURNICK.
1883. A. J. LURNICK.
1884. W. BROWN.

LIGHT WEIGHTS.

1881. F. W. HOBDAY.
1882. A. T. BETTINSON.
1883. A. DIAMOND.
1884. A. DIAMOND.

FEATHER WEIGHTS.

1881. T. HILL.
1882. T. HILL.
1883. T. HILL.
1884. W. HUTCHINGS.

BANTAM WEIGHT.

1884. A. WOODWARD.

AMATEUR BOXING CHAMPIONSHIPS.

QUEENSBERRY CHALLENGE CUPS.

CONDITIONS.

**Light Weight (25 Gns.). Middle Weight (30 Gns.)
Heavy Weight (35 Gns.).**

1. Competitors to box in a roped ring 24 feet square.

2. Competitors to box in light boots or shoes (without spikes), or in socks.

3. Weights to be—light, not exceeding 10 st.; middle, not exceeding 11 st. 4 lb.; heavy, any weight. Competitors to weigh on the day of competition.

4. The judging to be in the hands of three judges, whose decision in all cases shall be final. A timekeeper shall also be appointed.

5. In all open competitions the number of rounds to be contested shall be three. The duration of the first two rounds shall be three minutes, and of the final round four minutes, and the interval between each round shall be one minute.

6. In all competitions, any competitor failing to come up when time is called shall lose the bout.

7. Competitors to draw and weigh the day of competition. Whenever a competitor draws a bye he shall be bound to spar such bye for the specified time, and with such opponent as the judges may approve.

8. Each competitor shall be entitled to the assistance of one second only, and no advice or coaching shall be given to any competitor by his second, or by any other person, during the progress of any round.

9. The judges may caution or disqualify a competitor for infringing rules, or stop a round in the event of either man being knocked down; provided that the stopping of either of the first two rounds shall not disqualify any competitor from competing in the final round. And they may order a further round, limited to two minutes, should they think it necessary.

10. In all competitions the decision shall be given in favour of the competitor who displays the best style, and obtains the greatest number of points. The points shall be —for "Attack," direct clean hits with the knuckles of either hand, on any part of the front or sides of the head or body above the belt; "Defence," guarding, slipping, ducking, counter-hitting, or getting away. Where points are otherwise equal, consideration to be given to the man who does the most of the leading off.

11. The judges may, after cautioning the offender, disqualify a competitor who is boxing unfairly, by flicking or hitting with the open glove, by hitting with the inside or butt of the hand, the wrist, or elbow, or by wrestling, or roughing at the ropes.

12. In the event of any question arising not provided for in these rules, the judges and referee to have full power to decide such question or interpretation of rule.

13. The Cups to be boxed for once in each year, under the management of the A.A.C. (Trustees of the Cups), at Lillie Bridge.

DEFINITION OF AN AMATEUR.

An Amateur is one who has never competed with or against a Professional for any prize, and who has never taught, pursued, or assisted in the practice of athletic exercises as a means of obtaining a livelihood.

RULES

OF THE

AMATEUR BOXING ASSOCIATION.

---

1. In all open competitions the ring shall be roped, and of not less than 12 ft. or more than 24 ft. square.

2. Competitors to box in light boots or shoes (without spikes), or in socks, with knickerbockers, breeches, or trousers, and sleeved jerseys.

3. Weights to be—feather, not exceeding 9 st. ; light, not exceeding 10 st. ; middle, not exceeding 11 st. 4 lb. ; heavy, any weight. Competitors to weigh on the day of competition in boxing costume, without gloves.

4. In all open competitions the result shall be decided by two judges with a referee. A timekeeper shall be appointed.

5. In all open competitions the number of rounds to be contested shall be three. The duration of the first two rounds shall be three minutes, and of the final round four minutes, and the interval between each round shall be one minute.

6. In all competitions any competitor failing to come up when time is called shall lose the bout.

7. Where a competitor draws a bye, such competitor shall be bound to spar such bye for the specified time, and with such opponent as the judges of such competition may approve.

8. Each competitor shall be entitled to the assistance of one second only, and no advice or coaching shall be given to any competitor by his second, or by any other person, during the progress of any round.

9. The manner of judging shall be as follows :—The two judges and the referee shall be stationed apart. At the end of each bout each judge shall notify the name of the competitor, who, in his opinion, has won, and shall hand the same to an official appointed for the purpose. In the cases where the judges agree, such official shall announce the name of the winner ; but in cases where the judges disagree, such official shall so inform the referee, who shall thereupon himself decide.

10. The referee shall have power to give his casting vote when the judges disagree, or to stop a round in the event of either man being knocked down ; the stopping of either of the first two rounds shall not disqualify any competitor from competing in the final round. And he can order a further round, limited to two minutes, in the event of the judges disagreeing.

11. That the decision of the judges or referee, as the case may be, shall be final and without appeal.

12. In all competitions the decision shall be given in favour of the competitor who displays the best style and

obtains the greatest number of points. The points shall be —for "Attack," direct clean hits with the knuckles of either hand on any part of the front or sides of the head, or body above the belt; "Defence," guarding, slipping, ducking, counter-hitting, or getting away. Where points are otherwise equal, consideration to be given to the man who does most of the leading off.

13. The referee may, after cautioning the offender, disqualify a competitor who is boxing unfairly by flicking or hitting with the open glove, by hitting with the inside or butt of the hand, the wrist or elbow, or by wrestling, or roughing at the ropes.

14. In the event of any question arising not provided for in these rules, the judges and referee to have full power to decide such question or interpretation of rule.

QUEENSBURY CHAMPIONSHIP, 1884.

On April the 7th Lillie Bridge was again the scene of these championships, and the judges were the same as the previous year, viz. : — Messrs. BULPETT, MITCHELL, and GIBSON.

LIGHT-WEIGHT COMPETITION, not exceeding 10 st.

W. H. HEATH (Andover) beat C. A. BROOKES (Waite's School of Arms).

W. HUTCHINGS (St. James's A.C.) beat G. MAUDSLEY (Langham School of Arms, Manchester).

FINAL.—HUTCHINGS beat HEATH.—Round 1 : Heath led off with no effect, and Hutchings at once made play with both hands. Round 2 :· A slight improvement, and Hutchings appeared rather tired, but eventually scored fast. Round 3 : Heath commencing in good form, Hutchings at once set to work, both kept pegging away until " Time ! " was called, and Hutchings declared champion.

MIDDLE WEIGHTS, not exceeding 11 st 4 lb.

HARRY G. KINLOCH (Harrow-on-the-Hill) beat H. ARUNDEL (Stoke Newington).

F. EATON (Manchester) beat J. FOSTER (Notting Hill).

FINAL.—KINLOCH beat EATON.—Round 1 : Kinloch led off, and Eaton retaliated with three left-handers in succession. A series of spirited rallies ensued, and when hostilities ceased the points were prettily equally balanced. Round 2 : Both depended greatly on the left until a minute had expired, when Eaton made use of his right, but the bout was not particularly exciting. Round 3 : Kinloch sent in his left, and for the entire round nothing worthy of special comment occurred, and in the end another round of two minutes was ordered. Round 4 : No time was lost in the endeavour to make points fast, but neither sparred up to his usual form, the exchanges being wild and devoid of skill. Ultimately the verdict was in favour of Kinloch.

HEAVY WEIGHTS, any weight.

W. A. J. WEST (Northampton A.A.C.) beat F. WADE (Twickenham).—Round 1: West was considerably heavier and taller, and had the best of the first bout, but was very awkward. Round 2: Wade manifested improvement, and got well home with both hands, but weight told its inevitable tale towards the finish. Round 3: For the first minute Wade set about his man in magnificent style, but subsequently West knocked him down twice, amidst anything but approval from the audience, Wade being very weak, and finally the contest came to an abrupt conclusion, the latter receiving hearty applause from the company. Before leaving the ring Wade cordially shook West by the hand, and the pair retired in the most friendly fashion. This was the only contest as C. Phillips-Woolley (Waite's School of Arms) and Herbert Stevens (Salisbury) did not put in appearance.

AMATEUR BOXING ASSOCIATION.

Championship Judges:—B. J. Angle, Clapton Boxing Club; A. H. Curnick, West End School of Arms; Eugene Cox, Cestus Boxing Club; J. H. Douglas, Clapton Boxing Club; G. J. Garland, St. James's Athletic Club; E. A. Leigh, Manchester Boxing Club; A. T. Springbett, Clapton Boxing Club; W. Tailby, Birmingham Amateur Boxing Club; G. H. Vize, Clapton Boxing Club; R. Wakefield, Highbury Boxing Club.

This championship meeting took place on Wednesday, April 9th, 1884, at St. James's Hall, when the following competed:—

BANTAM WEIGHTS (8 st 4 lb and under).

FIRST ROUND.

E. Croysdill (G.G.S.) beat T. G. Walker (London)
H. J. Preston (W.L.B.C.) beat A. A. Jones (London)
A. Woodward (Birmingham) beat A. Bridge (St. James's A.C.)
A. Oates (London) beat W. A. Stevenson (London)
A. Lea (Birmingham B.C.) beat E. Goss (Westminster)

SECOND ROUND.

Preston beat Croysdill | Woodward a bye
Oates beat Lea

Third Round.

Woodward beat Preston | Oates a bye

Final.

Woodward beat Oates.

Counter-hits ensued as soon as the "chicks" got to work. In a very few seconds Woodward got merrily to work on the head and body, and eventually drew the claret. Oates showed signs of fatigue, but renewed each round in the gamest manner. At the finish Woodward planted on the forehead repeatedly, and won.

FEATHER WEIGHTS (9 st and under).

First Round.

H. Croysdill (G.G.S.) beat C. W. Monro (Cestus B.C.)
W. Newey (Birmingham B.C.) beat J. Shea (London)
H. Friswell (Royal Victor A.C.) beat G. Collier (Ivy Green A.B.C.)
E. Hutchings (18th Middlesex Rifles) beat T. J. M'Neill (London)

Second Round.

Croysdill beat Newey | Hutchings beat Friswell

Final.

Hutchings beat Croysdill.

In the first round Croysdill fairly stopped the rushes of the "rifleman," and ribbed him repeatedly. During the second, Hutchings tried the running-down tactics, but Croysdill proved very effective with both hands. We do not mean to infer that the veteran did not rub out a chalk or so in the wind up, but he certainly never got on terms with his adversary, who, we thought, ought to have gained the award.

LIGHT-WEIGHTS (10 st and under).

First Round.

D. J. Bacon (W.L.B.C.) beat J. Edmonds (Ivy Green A.B.C.)
G. Mawdsley (Langham School of Arms) beat W. Nunn (London)
E. Gobby (Eastern Central A.C.), a bye
A. Diamond (Birmingham B.C.), a bye

Second Round.

Diamond beat Gobby | Bacon beat Mawdsley

Final.

Diamond beat Bacon.

In the first and second rounds the men were well matched, but in the final round Bacon tired, and Diamond won with a lot in hand.

MIDDLE WEIGHTS (11 st 4 lb and under).

W. Brown (Birmingham B.C.) beat W. G. West (Northampton).

Brown had to concede a lot both in height and weight. Notwithstanding these disparities, he plumped in some thick-'uns with his left, and stopping cleverly, hampered his opponent considerably. West got home a swinging right-hander in the second bout, which appeared to tuck Brown up a-bit. He was soon at his man, though, and forcing the fighting, had chalked up the major portion of the points. In the concluding bout Brown got in his left twice without a reply, and stopping some well-directed blows with great agility, finally won with a bit in hand.

HEAVY WEIGHTS (no limit).

First Round.

W. A. J. West (Northampton) beat H. Keightley (Royal Victor A.A.C.)
H. T. Dearsley (St. James's A.C.) a bye with Jack Massey.

Final.

Dearsley beat West.

West, who showed signs of punishment went for Dearsley like a battering-ram, but the latter would not be caught napping, and getting in some "beauties," fairly knocked the Northampton representative out of time.

A Selection Of Classic Instructive Titles Relating To
The Art Of Pugilism & Self Defence
In Both War & Peace
Find our entire selection @ naval-military-press.com

ALL-IN FIGHTING
The distilled knowledge of W.E. Fairbairn, legendary SOE instructor in unarmed combat, and inventor of the Sykes-Fairbairn knife, who learned his deadly skills in 30 years on the Shanghai waterfront.
Fully illustrated.
9781847348531

ART OF BOXING AND SCIENCE OF SELF DEFENCE
Former Lightweight Champion Billy Edwards shares the techniques and strategies of the sweet science in his beautifully illustrated boxing guide. Explore boxing's transition from bare knuckle spectacle to today's Marquis of Queensbury ruleset.
9781474539548

JACK GOODWIN'S BOXING
This 1920's boxing masterpiece by Jack Goodwin puts you in the shoes of a coach in that era. Uncover the best ways to run, manage and train boxers as taught by Jack Godwin, a champion and trainer of champions in the noble science.
9781474539586

ART OF WRESTLING
George de Relwyskow Army Gymnastic Staff
In the appreciation to this book Captain Daniels, V.C., M.C., Rifle Brigade, states: "In adding a word to this book on the style of wrestling as taught at the Headquarters Gymnasium of the British Army, and having had personal experience in the various holds and throws taught, I consider it has been of great value in the training of the soldier, and the bringing out of those qualities of grit and determination which have been seen in all ranks who have taken an active part throughout the greatest war in history." 1919.
9781783313563

THE COMPLETE BOXER
Gunner Moir provides detailed instructions on the techniques he deployed to become British Heavyweight Champion. Taught in a series of easy to learn techniques, combinations, and boxing strategies.
9781474539609

BOXING (V-Five)
The Aviation Training Office of the Chief of Naval Operations
The game-changing V-Five suite of training manuals helped get a generation of American aviators fit for war. Here we explore how the airmen of the US navy trained in boxing as part of their military fitness regime.
9781474539623

WRESTLING (V-Five)
The Aviation Training Office of the Chief of Naval Operations

The game-changing V-Five suite of training manuals helped get a generation of American aviators fit for war. Here we explore how the airmen of the US navy trained in collegiate wrestling as part of their military fitness regime.

9781474539685

THE TEXTBOOK OF WRESTLING

Get your wrestling skills matt-ready from wrestling champion and world-renown trainer Ernest Gruhn. Replete with detailed holds, throws, pins and strategies for success in a wide range of wrestling rulesets.

9781474539647

KILL OR GET KILLED

Rex Applegate's "kill or be killed" helped prepare America's marines, soldiers, sailors, spies and airmen for the realities of war. This highly shared and respected work provides all you need to know about unarmed combat and close quarter engagement with the enemy.

9781474539661

MANUAL OF PHYSICAL TRAINING 1914
(United States Army)

Published just prior to the outbreak of World War 1, this beautifully illustrated guide was designed to revolutionise the combat fitness and readiness of the US Army covering a wide range of gymnastic and combat calisthenic exercises.

DEAL THE FIRST DEADLY BLOW
United States Department of the Army

This Vietnam-era classic showcases in detail how the US Forces trained in close quarter combat. Known as the "encyclopaedia of combat" it helped a generation learn how to become devastating effective with empty hands, knives and bayonets alike.

9781474539722

HAND-TO-HAND COMBAT
Bureau of Aeronautics U.S Navy 1943

This is one of the best combative manuals from World War 2, developed by the US Navy V-Five Staff, that included the renowned American wrestler Wesley Brown. It is then not especially surprising that wrestling skills predominate in this manual, and form the base skill-set for this combative system.

9781474537391

ABWEHR ENGLISCHER GANGSTER METHODEN DEFENSE OF ENGLISH GANGSTERS METHODS – SILENT KILLING – FULL ENGLISH TRANSLATION

In 1942 the Wehrmacht published a training manual with the goal of countering the "silent killing" tactics used by the British commando units. The manual was – much in line with typical National Socialist terminology –titled

"Abwehr Englischer Gangster-methoden" or "Defence Against English Gangster methods".

This book was compiled due the Wehrmacht intelligence operatives uncovering of a British hand-to-hand course for the SOE, Commandos, et al, on methods of quick and silent killing (undoubtedly developed by W. E. Fairbairn and E. A. Sykes). They correctly assessed that their troops in general and particularly the Geheime Staatspolizei (Gestapo), Sicherheitsdienst (SD), their security guards, and sentries would be in grave danger when confronted by men trained in these methods. This manual/program was the Wehrmacht's response.

9781474538336

HAND TO HAND COMBAT

Francois d'Eliscu taught thousands of U.S. Army Rangers how to fight down and dirty in World War II.d'Eliscu doesn't get the press that Fairbairn and Applegate do, but he did a commendable job writing this book,It is basic, meant for training raw recruits in a short amount of time before sending them to the front, but simple is good when you are in combat, as most combative experts' will tell you.

9781474535823

WE Fairbairn's Complete Compendium of Lethal, Unarmed, Hand-to-Hand Combat Methods and Fighting In Colour

All 844 images of Fairbairn and his assistants can now for the first time be seen in full colour, lending a clarity to the practical methods of mastering the manner of dealing with an assailant, both in time of war and when placed in difficulty during unpleasant modern urban situations. These various holds, trips, kicks, blows etc, allow the average man or woman a position of security against almost any form of armed or unarmed attack.

Captain W.E. Fairbairn would have approved of this new colour version, that gives an illustrative clarity to the original that was lacking in previous monochrome reprints of his work.

All six of W.E. Fairbairn's works in one binding to create the ultimate colour compendium: Get Tough-All-In Fighting-Shooting to Live-Scientific Self-Defence-Hands Off!-Defendu

9781783318735

BOXING FOR BOYS
Regtl. Sergt.-Major E B Dent Army Gymnastic Headquarters
A successful system of boxing instruction for large classes, to allow tuition with no detriment to the "backward or shy pupil". Covers Kit-On, Guard-Sparring-Advance-Point & Mark-Ducking-Medicine, Bag-Left & Right Hooks etc. The author considered that boxing systematically taught to the youth was beneficial exercise, and would have a marked elevating influence on the national character.
9781783314607

HAND-TO-HAND FIGHTING
A System Of Personal Defence For The Soldier (1918)
A tough book on the art of hand to hand fighting in the trenches of the Great War. Demonstrating techniques utilised to "do away with the enemy", many of which are barred in clean wrestling, the book includes good clear photographic illustrations presenting important attack methods including the "Hammer Lock", "Kidney Kick", "Head Twist", "Knee Groin Kick", and the "Knee Break", all very important in a man to man, life or death encounter, when fighting in the mud of the trenches.
9781783313983

www.ingramcontent.com/pod-product-compliance
Lightning Source LLC
Chambersburg PA
CBHW070459100426
42743CB00010B/1682